DINGFEST

Ernst Jandl

THINGSURE

translated from the German by

Michael Hamburger

DEDALUS

POETRY EUROPE SERIES No. 2

THE DEDALUS PRESS
24 The Heath,
Cypress Downs,
Dublin 6W
Ireland

ISBN 1 901233 11 1

Dedalus Press books are distributed in the U.K. by
Password (Books) Ltd., 23 New Mount St., Manchester
M4 4DE, and in the U.S.A. and Canada by Dufour
Editions Inc., PO Box 7, Chester Springs, Pennsylvania
19425 - 0007

This translation has been financially supported by the
Bundesministerium für Wissenschaft, Forschung und
Kunst in Vienna/Austria.

The Dedalus Press receives financial assistance from
An Chomhairle Ealaíon, The Arts Council, Ireland

Printed by Colour Books Ltd., Dublin

CONTENTS

INTRODUCTION

This small selection from one kind of poem written by Ernst Jandl over the decades can still be no more than a belated introduction to his work for English-language readers. There was a time, in the 'sixties and early 'seventies, when no such introduction would have been needed, because Jandl was known in Britain as a brilliant speaker of his performance poems, appearing at international poetry readings like those at the Albert Hall, on the radio, and in print, in two small books put out by Bob Cobbing and the Turret Bookshop respectively. Apart from a fringe staging of his 'opera for speaking voices', *Out Of Estrangement*, at the Edinburgh Festival of 1985 – and a printing of my version of it in the Cambridge University Press yearbook *Comparative Criticism* – Jandl has ceased to be present here as a poet, playwright or performer ever since.

In his own country, Austria, too, he was widely marginalized, maligned or ignored as long as that was compatible with political-cum-cultural correctness. For his sixtieth birthday in 1985, however, a three-volume collected works edition was issued by a major German publisher, followed by at least six CD recordings of his readings, with or without music, and by three large collections of later poems. The poems in the collected works edition alone fill more than sixteen-hundred pages; and the third volume adds more than seven hundred pages of dramatic works and miscellaneous prose.

Throughout the decades, repeatedly, I have tried to draw attention to the distinction of Ernst Jandl's work, and cannot do so here without repeating myself once more. This distinction lies in Jandl's capacity to reconcile what, elsewhere, are the extreme polarities of poetic practice, between 'pure' or 'concrete' verse at the one end, a reductive representationalism at the other. What is common to both procedures is his workmanlike application to the material, language and application that has not flagged even when he was

5

beset by the 'yellow dog', depression. From this depression in turn he wrested almost daily defiances of the blankness that was its effect. Yet only one end of his range is represented in my selection. That is why something must be said about the whole gamut, though Jandl himself has given a full and exemplary account of it in two books of workshop reports, *die schöne kunst des schreibens* (the fine art of writing) 1976, enlarged edition 1983, and *das öffnen und schliessen des mundes* (the opening and shutting of the mouth), 1985. Needless to say, these, too, have never appeared in English, though I know of no contribution to poetics at once so personal and so comprehensive, so penetrating and so unpretentiously plain.

Jandl emerged as a writer of 'conventional' poems (those in 'every-day language and normal grammar') – in 1956, but soon became associated with the Vienna Art Club and the Vienna Group of experimental writers. In fact, from the start, it was the tension between the poem as verbal artefact and the poem as vehicle for communication that opened up all the various possibilities Jandl has pursued. His next two books were published in Stuttgart and Frauenfeld, the two headquarters of experimental and 'concrete' writing in German at the time, his fourth, with the Anglo-German or Jinglish title *mai hart lieb zapfen eibe hold*, in London. English had become important to Jandl when he was a prisoner-of-war. A later stay followed when he had become a teacher of English, which he remained until he became a free-lance writer in 1976. Right up to his most recent book, Jandl has written a good many poems in English, including this comment on his anomalous and seemingly irreconcilable practices:

i love concrete
i love pottery
but i'm not
a concrete pot

There is more to this tiny squib than the knowledge that he is a poet not to be placed or categorized except in and on his own terms. Much as composers of music were once known as 'tone-setters', before Beethoven objected to the artisan status implied in that term, whatever else he was or did, Jandl has always been a craftsman above all, a setter, potter or turner of words. As such, he has reversed the Romantic-Symbolist revolution, thoroughly breaking with its vatic stances and ambitions. Content to be a maker, he was free to make this or that, more often than not something that was both this and that. Thus his own first kind of poem, that in conventional or representational language, is sub-divided in his later work by poems in what he calls 'deteriorated' or sub-literary diction – which was taken to be a sort of guest worker pidgin, but, to him, is a child-like medium – and poems in Viennese dialect. His 'Sprechgedichte', poems for reading aloud, have a similar range and diversity, including the Jinglish already mentioned, as in his famous 'calypso', which neither permits nor needs translation and begins:

ich was not yet
in brasilien
nach brasilien
wulld ich laik du go

wer de wimmen
arr so ander
so quait ander
denn anderwo . . .

Here the phonetics of the fourth line also attest to his native Viennese dialect, in that standard German would demand 'tu' in place of 'du'.

The third kind, his 'Lautgedicht' or sound poem, can also overlap with the second; and even his most rigorously pure sound poems can carry a message, no less than those of his first and second kind. His most immediately popular performance poems were those like 'schmerz durch reibung' (pain through friction) made out of the sounds in the single word 'frau'; or 'schtzngrmm' (trench), made out of the consonants only in the German word 'Schützengraben' – in its Viennese pronunciation once more. Poems of that kind need to be heard rather than read, since the letters on the page are a notation more difficult to take in through the eye than a musical score; and, because no one but the poet could vocalize them exactly as they were meant to be vocalized, a small record of his reading was issued together with the text. Thus the last line of 'schtzngrmm' – 't-tt' – looks like an onomatopoeic enactment of rifle or machine-gun fire, but the dying fall of Jandl's reading of it recalls the missing vowel of the German word 'tot'. Perhaps only Jandl's fourth kind of poem, the silent visual one, qualifies as a pure artefact without the usefulness of pots as containers or of the building material, concrete.

Another outstanding early performance poem fuses neologistic wordplay with social and psychological comment as trenchant as any by Brecht – with the implication that Brecht's unalienated diction could have been a vehicle too rational for phenomena like that of Jandl's poem, the jubilant reception given to Hitler on his entry into annexed Austria's capital. This poem belongs to the untranslatable sort, but my imitation or travesty goes like this :

Vienna: heldenplatz

the glintire heldenplatz just about
was subsplurged in a mesh-like human flood
women too amongst it who to the muscle-knee
to weld themselves wildly strove, pregnant with hope.
and roared substantially.

bravouring brow-parting's underswing
from needs, notes northern, hackled
with a number-swell blood-lusting voice
that scythed all home-launderers flat.

at 'em!
the goddlebuck drabbled from phra-ase to phra-ase
with a mucho spriff vocal stub.
Ruttily a writhing rose in the mannekin flood
and the women so whitsunly felt their salvation
espicily when a knee-ender staggled them.

Art, for Jandl, is 'the perpetual implementation of a freedom', a freedom he has maintained for himself by access to a whole field of the different kinds of writing he has chosen or been impelled to do. Far from being taken in by 'the demon of progress in the arts' (Wyndham Lewis), though, Jandl has not even claimed a personal 'development' for himself. "Merely by writing poems", he has stated, "the experimental poet 'continues a tradition', a tradition that consists of many traditions"; but also, much more astonishingly: "By the time I was 9 years old I had written my first poem. I still stand in the same place."

This remark becomes understandable in the light of Jandl's later work. Another biographical aside in his writings reveals that in his adolescence he had wished to be a priest. Some of his latest poems bear out both these statements, astonishing as they remain to those shocked by the profanities and indecencies at the other end of Jandl's intransigent truth-telling both in verbally playful works and in the dead-on reports on experience that have come to preponderate in his later books. More than ten years ago, in a TLS review, I pointed to the poem 'das schöne bild', as one that stood out from all the others in his collection *selbstporträt des schachspielers als trinkende uhr* (self-portrait of the chess-player as a drinking clock) of 1983. Its quotation from the liturgical version of St. Matthew 8,8 – words recalled from an early Communion service, as Jandl has indicated – offer a clue to all the seeming contradictions in his practice. The beautiful picture of this poem has to be an abstract one – and, paradoxically, abstract in painting corresponds to 'concrete' in poetry – so as to exclude everything human. Jandl's poems of human experience, on the other hand, engage with a fallen condition, going out of their way to be anything but beautiful or edifying. (Here it must be remembered that Jandl grew up under a concordat between his Church and the Third Reich. His poem 'vienna : heldenplatz' makes the connection.) I leave the aesthetic and theological implication to others, but have said enough to suggest why Jandl chose to be a poet of the lower case, as funny as he is serious and sad, as popular as he is demanding and uncompromising. The lower regions he has chosen to chart in most of his later verse have a complement of commitment and faith that usually remains implicit. (A few explicit pointers to it have been included in this book.)

Just because Jandl does not attach any exemplary importance to his person or individuality, he has been able to draw freely (once more) on the most trivial, every-day and sordid occurrences of his own life – most remarkably in his minutely realistic but verbally distanced play or 'opera for speaking voices' about his long-standing, but also distant association with the poet and prose writer Friederike Mayröcker. The distancing in this play was achieved by the resort to reported speech in the dialogue. Yet for Austrian stagings the main characters were chosen for their physical resemblance to Jandl and Mayröcker respectively. Only Jandl could have written a play at once so self-exposing and so far from being mawkish. His own life happens to be what Jandl knows best. As for detachment, language, as wrought by him in whatever mode is appropriate to the matter, takes care of that.

One-sided as my selection is, being confined to short poems of all periods, yet of only the straight kind most congenial to a translator never mistaken for a concrete pot – though also compelled at times to produce what I call 'unpleasantries' or 'owl's pellets' – it may serve to break the ice. Other translators are likely to complement it with versions of the longer, more verbally inventive texts, not least because few readers can respond to the whole of Jandl's incomparable range. Yet, as I have tried to intimate without the bibliographical or analytical elaboration that would overbuden a brief text, all Jandl's modes can be traced to a single source and a centre very firmly fixed.

Michael Hamburger
Suffolk, March 1997

Stilleben

Ich habe meined Kugelschreiber, der rot-blau schreibt,
auf die Zündholzschachtel gelegt.
Das ist aufregend wie die Feuerwehr,
verglichen mit dem Schreibpapier daneben.

Das gleang mir nach dem Versuch,
einen großartigen Gedanken zu haben.
(Ein Blatt Papier starb dabei an einem Ausschlag
von häßlichen blauen Buchstaben.

Sich zu erinnern

Jung und gefangen
hinter Stacheldraht
auf einem Quadrat aus Lehm
für hundert Mann,
begann er bei Nacht
auf dem Weg zwischen Zelt und Latrine
sich zu errinern an
die Sichtbarkeit der Sterne.

Jung und zurückgekehrt
in seine Heimat
auf ein Holzquadrat
für sieben Köpfe,
begann er bei Nacht
im Schlaf zwischen Hunger und Kälte
sich zu errinern an
die Fruchtbarkeit der Ferne.

Still Life

I have laid my ball-pen which writes
red or blue on the matchbox.
That is thrilling as the fire engine
compared with the sheet of paper beside it.

I succeeded in that after trying
to have a magnificent thought.
(In the process a sheet of paper
died of a rash of ugly blue letters.)

To Remember

Young and imprisoned
behind barbed wire
on a patch of clay
for a hundred men,
at night, on his way
from tent to latrine
he began to remember
the visibility of stars.

Young and returned
to his home town,
on a wooden patch
for seven persons,
at night, asleep
between hunger and cold
he began to remember
the fruitfulness of places afar.

Im Schlaf

Er traf einen Baum.
Er baute darunter sein Haus.
Er schnitt aus dem Baum
einen Stock heraus.
Der Stock wurde seine Lanze.
Die Lanze wurde sein Gewehr.
Das Gewehr wurde seine Kanone.
Die Kanone wurde seine Bombe.
Die Bombe traf sein Haus und riß
den Baum an den Wurzeln aus.
Er stand dabei und staunte,
aber auf wachte er nicht.

zweierlei handzeichen

ich bekreuzige mich
vor jeder kirche
ich bezwetschkige mich
vor jedem obstgarten

wie ich ersteres tue
weiß jeder katholik
wie ich letzteres tue
ich allein

Asleep

He came across a tree.
He built his house beneath it.
Out of the tree he cut
himself a stick.
The stick became his lance.
The lance became his rifle.
The rifle became a cannon.
The cannon became a bomb.
The bomb hit his house and ripped
up the tree by the roots.
He stood there wondering
but he didn't wake up.

two kinds of signs

i cross myself
in front of every church
i plum myself
in front of every orchard

how i do the former
every catholic knows
how i do the latter
i alone

lied

schlaf gut für mich
bis morgen
schlaf für mich;
schlaf für mich
denn ich möchte dich jetzt.
schlaf gut für mich
bis morgen
schlaf für mich;
schlaf für mich
denn du kannst erst morgen.
schlaf gut für mich
bis morgen
schlaf für mich,
denn ich möchte dich jetzt
und du kannst erst morgen.
schlaf gut für mich
bis morgen
schlaf für mich,
denn du kannst erst morgen
und jetzt ist die liebe.

song

sleep well for me
till tomorrow
sleep for me;
sleep for me,
for i want you now.
sleep well for me
till tomorrow
sleep for me
for you can't till tomorrow.
sleep well for me
till tomorrow
sleep for me,
for i want you now
and you can't till tomorrow.
sleep well for me
till tomorrow
sleep for me,
for you can't till tomorrow
and love is now.

anfrage

ich schickte meinen namen aus der stadt
in telegrammen, und fuhr hinterher.

der zug der mich herauszog aus der stadt
blieb im geleise.

ich schickte meinen namen in die stadt
in telegrammen, und fuhr hinterher.

der zug der mich zurückzog in die stadt
blieb im geleise.

wo blieb die reise?

sieben kinder

wieviele kinder haben sie eigentlich? – sieben
zwei von der ersten frau
zwei von der zweiten frau
zwei von der dritten frau
und eins
ein ganz kleins
von mir selber

question

i sent my name out of the city
in telegrams, and followed them.

the train that took me out of the city
remained on the rails.

i sent my name into the city
in telegrams, and followed them.

the train that took me back into the city
remained on the rails.

what became of the trip?

seven children

how many children do you have, then? – seven
two by my first wife
two by my second wife
two by my third wife
and one
a very tiny one
by myself

taschen

schau, meine vielen taschen.
in dieser hab ich ansichtskarten.

in dieser zwei uhren.
meine zeit und deine zeit.

in dieser einen würfel.
23 augen sehen mehr als zwei.

du kannst dir denken
was ich an brillen schleppe.

'einfach ...'

einfach
ein tag
eine nacht

es hüpft mich
vom einen
zum andern

es wächst mich
es wacht mich
es schläft mich

es lebt mich
vom einen
zur einen

tag

nacht

pockets

look, all those pockets of mine.
in this one i keep picture postcards.

in this one two watches.
my time and your time.

in this one a die.
23 eyes see more than two.

you can imagine
how many pairs of glasses i lug around.

'simply . . .'

simply
one day
one night

it hops me
from one
to the next

it grows me
it wakes me
it sleeps me

it lives me
from one
to the one

day

night

urteil

die gedichte dieses mannes sind unbrauchbar.

zunächst
rieb ich eines in meine glatze.
vergeblich. es förderte nicht meinen haarwuchs.

daraufhin
betupfte ich mit einem meine pickel. diese
erreichten binnen zwei tagen die größe mittlerer kartoffeln.
die ärzte staunten.

daraufhin
schlug ich zwei in die pfanne.
etwas mißtrauisch, aß ich nicht selber.
daran starb mein hund.

daraufhin
benützte ich eines als schutzmittel.
dafür zahlte ich die abtreibung.

daraufhin
klemmte ich eines ins auge
und betrat einen besseren klub.
der portier
stellte mir ein bein, daß ich hinschlug.

daraufhin
fällte ich obiges urteil.

judgement

this man's poems are good for nothing.

for a start
i rubbed one of them into my bald scalp.
in vain, it didn't make my hair grow.

then
with one of them i dabbed my pimples. these
within two daws attained the size of a medium potato.
the doctors were amazed.

then
i cracked two of them into the frying-pan.
a bit suspicious, i didn't eat them myself.
but my dog died from them.

then
i used one as a contraceptive.
that cost me the price of an abortion.

then
i wedged one into an eye
and entered an exclusive club.
the porter
tripped me up, so that i fell down flat.

then
i pronounced the above judgement.

dingfest

auf einem stuhl
liegt ein hut.
beide
wissen voneinander
nichts.
beide
sind
so dingfest

im delicatessenladen

bitte geben sie mir eine maiwiesenkonserve
etwas höher gelegen aber nicht zu anschüssig
so, daß man darauf noch sitzen kann.

nun, dann vielleicht eine schneehalde, tiefgekühlt
ohne wintersportler. eine fichte schön beschneit
kann dabeisein.

auch nicht. bliebe noch – hasen sehe ich haben sie da hängen.
zwei drei werden genügen. und natürlich einen jäger.
wo hängen denn die jäger?

zwei in einem

mein rock hat keine unbekannten taschen.
ich schreibe nicht mit unsichtbarer tinte.
meine brillen zeigen nicht, was hinter mir geschieht.

ich finde meine finger in fremden taschen.
ich lese papiere, die jeder für leer hält.
ich schaue dir in die augen und sehe die sintflut hinter mir.

thingsure

on a chair
lies a hat.
neither
knows anything
of the other.
both
are
so thingsure

at the delicatessen shop

please give me a potted may meadow
a slightly higher altitude but not too steep
so that one can still sit on it.

all right, then, maybe a snowy slope, deep-frozen
but no skiers, please. a fir tree beautifully snowed on
can be thrown in.

you haven't? that leaves – i see you have hares hanging there.
two or three should be enough. and a huntsman of course.
where do you hang them? i don't see the huntsmen.

two in one

my jacket has no unknown pockets.
i do not write in invisible ink.
my spectacles don't show me what happens behind my back.

i find my fingers in strange people's pockets.
i read sheets of paper that everyone tells me are blank.
i look into your eyes and see the flood behind my back.

25

jeder sein edison

im nest der taufologie
behagt es jedem. kautomation
verspricht lebenslängliche atzung. kraftologie
ist die einzige wissenschaft. telefant
trägt jeden zu jedem, telekraft
ebenso. lyrkitsch und krankophon
beschäftigen drüsen und ohren. orden aus quarzinom
verleiht der präsident der u.s.w.

vorsicht: frisch gestrichen

vom stuhl zu boden geworfen
vom boden zur decke geschleudert
von der decke an die wand geklatscht
von der wand gegens fenster geboxt
vom fenster auf die straße geflippt
von der straße aufs dach gekickt
vom dach in die luke gestopft
von her luke ins gebälk gerotzt
vom gebälk auf die bretter gerammt
von den brettern zur treppe geprügelt
von der treppe auf den flur geschottert
vom flur durch die tür gestaucht
von der tür auf den boden gespien
vom boden auf den stuhl geschmiert

every man his own edison

in the nest of mistology
everybody feels snug. eatomation
promsies lifelong fodder. powerology
is the only science. telephant
carries each to each, telepower
likewise. lyrekitsch and sickophone
occupy glands and ears. quarcinoma medals
are awarded by the president of the e.t.c.

wet paint!

chucked on the floor from the chair
hurled from the floor to the ceiling
splashed from the ceiling to the wall
punched from the wall against the window
flicked from the window onto the street
kicked from the street onto the roof
stuffed from the roof into the skylight
snotted from the skylight into the rafters
rammed from the rafters onto the boards
flogged from the boards onto the staircase
strewn from the staircase into the vestibule
jammed from the vestibule through the door
spewed from the door onto the floor
smeared from the floor onto the chair

das hemd

wirkt
dieses hemd schon dreckig, ist
nicht die frage; sie ist
ist dieses hemd schon dreckig.

ist
dieses hemd schon dreckig, ist
nicht die frage; sie ist
wirkt dieses hemd schon dreckig.

kühlschrank

er onaniert
ununterbrochen.
es zittert das ganze haus.

abhilfe:
man schleicht sich an,
reißt die tür auf
– sofort
hört er auf.
man schlägt die tür zu;
einige zeit bleibt ruh.

the shirt

does
this shirt look dirty already is
not the question; it is
is this shirt dirty already

is this shirt dirty already is
not the question; it is
does this shirt look dirty already.

refrigerator

it masturbates
incessantly.
the whole house shakes.

remedy:
you creep up to it,
rip open the door
– at once
it will cease.
you slam the door;
for a while there is peace.

von namen

ich weiß ja nicht mehr, was ein name ist
aber angeschnallt bin an einen solchen ich auch
und die großen philosophen und die dichter auch
hatten einen solchen, ebenso die feldherren
und die könige und kaiser und die tribünen
nur die tribünen kamen mit einer nummer aus
und ohne namen und nummer die bienen

nein ich wollte keine biene sein, denn ihr fleiß
ist meine sache nicht, aber eine birne
sein wollte ich schon, die gebissen wird
von schönen weißen zähnen und heraus rinnt
birnensaft über bärtige kinne, aber innen
klein und schwarz trägt sie die bilder aller
birnbäume namenlos, ein volk von hoffnung

weh wenn ertappt ich werden sollte als namen-süchtig
den ich nicht selbst mir gab und der herausgekratzt
werden muß wie ein dreimonatiger foetus, der nie
benannt wird werden und der genug an zeit hat
gehabt für sein wachsen; so verrotte ich
gern auch unbegraben auf diesem verfluchten stern
wenn meinen namen ich endlich vergessen kann

of names

well, i no longer know what a name might be
but all the same i too am fixed to one
and great philosophers and the poets too
had names attached, likewise the generals
the kings and emperors, as did the tribunes
only the tribunes could make do with numbers
and with no name or number so can the bees

no, never did i wish to be a bee, because
their industry is not my thing, but a ripe pear
i'd like to be, a pear that's bitten
by beautiful white teeth, from which runs out
pear juice on bearded chins, although within
tiny and black it bears the image of
all peartrees namelessly, a people of hope

woe if i were caught red-handed as the addict to
a name i did not give myself, to be
scraped out like a three-month-old foetus which
never will have a name and has had time enough
for that much growth; thus readily, if need be,
i'd putrify unburied on this damned star
if then at last i could forget my name

der mann von nebenan

du siehst ihn nicht
du kennst ihn nicht
du weißt nicht was sein zustand ist
ich seh ihn nicht
ich kenn ihn nicht
ich weiß nicht was sein zustand ist
oder sieht ihn wer?
oder kennt ihn wer?
oder weiß wer was sein zustand ist?
man sieht ihn nicht
man kennt ihn nicht
man weiß nicht was sein zustand ist

das wappen

wenn Sie mich fragen – ich
brauche längst
keine gedichte mehr

ein nichtrauchender trafikant
ein abstinenter schnapsbrenner

nein gewiß
mein wappen
enthält das bett
und die flasche

kein buch
keine feder
kein blatt

the man next door

you don't see him
you don't know him
you don't know how he is or fares
i don't see him
i don't know him
i don't know how he is or fares
or does anyone see him?
or does anyone know him?
or does anyone know how he is or fares?
one doesn't see him
one doesn't know him
one doesn't know how he is or fares

the coat of arms

if you ask me – i've long
ceased to need
poems

a non-smoking tobacconist
a teetotal distiller

no for sure
my coat of arms
contains the bed
and the bottle

no book
no pen
no paper

nichts und etwas

nichts im kopf
setze ich mich
an die maschine
spanne ein blatt ein
mit nichts darauf

mit etwas darauf
ziehe das blatt ich
aus der maschine
und lese als text
etwas aus meinem kopf

der nagel

festnageln ich will
diesen da tag, jeden da
jeden da tag da fest
nageln ich will daß nicht
mehr er entkomme mir daß nicht
mir er entkomme mehr daß nicht
einer entkomme mir mehr nicht ein
einziger mehr mir entkomme wie
vorher als so viele ich nicht
festgenagelt habe mit gedicht

nothing and something

nothing in my head
i sit down
at the typewriter
insert a sheet
with nothing on it

with something on it
i extract the sheet
from the typewriter
and read as a text
something out of my head

the nail

nail down i will
this here day, every here
every here day here nail
down i will so that
it shall not slip away again
not slip away from me so that
not one shall slip away not one
single day slip away from me as
before when so many i did not
nail down with poem one jot

my own song

ich will nicht sein
so wie ihr mich wollt
ich will nicht ihr sein
so wie ihr mich wollt
ich will nicht sein wie ihr
so wie ihr mich wollt
ich will nicht sein wie ihr seid
so wie ihr mich wollt
ich will nicht sein wie ihr sein wollt
so wie ihr mich wollt

nicht wie ihr mich wollt
wie ich sein will will ich sein
nicht wie ihr mich wollt
wie ich bin will ich sein
nicht wie ihr mich wollt
wie *ich* will ich sein
nicht wie ihr mich wollt
ich will *ich* sein
nicht wie ihr mich wollt will ich sein
ich will *sein*.

my own song

i don't want to be
as you would have me be
i don't want to be you
as you would have me be
i don't want to be like you
as you would have me be
i don't want to be as you are
as you would have me be
i don't want to be what you want to be
as you would have me be

not as you want me
to be i i want to be
not as you want me
as i am i want to be
not as you want me
like me i want to be
not as you want me
i want to be i
not as you want me i want to be
i want to *be*.

woran ich jetzt arbeite

woran ich jetzt arbeite
daran arbeite ich jetzt
beantworte ich unausgesetzt
die frage eines jeden

ich beantworte unausgesetzt
die frage eines jeden
woran ich jetzt arbeite.
daran arbeite ich jetzt

stück für zwei hände

die rechte hand klatscht
die linke hand klatscht
beide hände klatschen

die rechte hand klatscht in die rechte hand
die linke hand klatscht in die linke hand
beide hände klatschen in beide hände

beide hände klatschen in die rechte hand
beide hände klatschen in die linke hand
jede hand klatscht in beide hände

ohne rechte hand klatschen
ohne linke hand klatschen
ohne hände klatschen

what i'm working on now

what i'm working on now
is what i'm working on now
i keep answering
everyone's question

i keep answering
everyone's question
what i'm working on now.
that's what i'm working on now

piece for two hands

the right hand claps
the left hand claps
both hands clap

the right hand claps into the right hand
the left hand claps into the left hand
both hands clap into both hands

both hands clap into the right hand
both hands clap into the left hand
each hand claps into both hands

clap without the right hand
clap without the left hand
clap without hands

der verlorene sohn

sohn! sohn!
ruft der vater
den verlorenen sohn

vater! vater!
ruft nach dem vater
der verlorene sohn

sohn! sohn!
ruft die mutter
den verlorenen sohn

mutter! mutter!
ruft nach der mutter
der verlorene sohn

bruder! bruder!
ruft die schwester
den verlorenen sohn

schwester! schwester!
ruft nach der schwester
der verlorene sohn

bruder! bruder!
ruft der bruder
den verlorenen sohn

bruder! bruder!
ruft nach dem bruder
der verlorene sohn

the prodigal son

son! son!
the father calls out
for the prodigal son

father! father!
for his father calls out
the prodigal son

son! son!
the mother calls out
for the prodigal son

mother! mother!
for his mother calls out
the prodigal son

borther! brother!
his siter calls out
for the prodigal son

sister! sister!
for his sister calls out
the prodigal son

brother! brother!
his brother calls out
for the prodigal son

brother! brother!
for his brother calls out
the prodigal son

hilfe! hilfe!
rufen schließlich
alle

hilfe! hilfe!
rufen schließlich
alle

während

im anfang
die erde
war wüst
und leer

aber blühend
und voll
wird sie sein

während du
sie verläßt

help! help!
in the end
all of them call

help! help!
in the end
all of them call

while

in the beginning
the earth
was waste
and bare

but flowering
and rich
it will be

while you
depart from it

doppelt so weit

ich bin neu auf der welt
und ich geh von mir weg
und ich geh zu mir hin
ich bin sechs monate
unc ich geh von mir weg
und ich geh zu mir hin
ich bin ein jahr alt
und ich geh von mir weg
und ich geh zu mir hin
wie ich zwei jahre bin
und ich geh von mir weg
und ich geh zu mir hin
das ist mein vierter geburtstag
und ich geh von mir weg
und ich geh zu mir hin
als ein schulkind von acht jahren
und ich geh von mir weg
und ich geh zu mir hin
und erkenne mich mit sechzehn kaum wieder
und ich geh von mir weg
und ich geh zu mir hin
der zweiunddreißigste ist ein schöner geburtstag
und ich geh von mir weg
und ich geh zu mir hin
ich mit vierundsechzig
geh nicht mehr doppelt so weit

twice as far

i am new to the world
and i go away from myself
and i go towards myself
i am six months old
and i go away from myself
and i go towards myself
i am one year old
and i go away from myself
and i go towards myself
this is my fourth birthday
and i go away from myself
and i go towards myself
as a schoolboy of eight
and i go away from myself
and i go towards myself
and at sixteen i scarcely recognize myself
and i go away from myself
and i go towards myself
the thirty-second is a fine birthday
and i go away from myself
and i go towards myself
at sixty-four i
no longer go twice as far

inhalt

um ein gedicht zu machen
habe ich nichts

eine gaze sprache
ein ganzes leben
ein ganzes denken
ein ganzes erinnern

um ein gedicht zu machen
habe ich nichts

falsch

hier tut kein weg sein
und ich tu ihn auch nicht suchen
ich tu was ich tu was ich tun müssen tu
immer sein da die die sagen
das du müssen tun und das du müssen tun
und ich sein das was da ja sagen tut
ja ich immer tu ja sagen
und dann ich mir sagen da falsch
war das jasagen
ja
ganz falsch

gist

for the making of a poem
i have nothing

a whole language
a whole life
a whole thinking
a whole remembering

for the making of a poem
i have nothing

wrong

here there be no way
nor do i look for it either
i do what i do what do i must
always there be them who say
this you must do and that you must do
and i be him who do say yes
yes always i do say yes
and then i do say to myself it was wrong
this yes-saying
yes
quite wrong

unsagbar

so voll
gefüllt
von nicht
sagbarem
un-
sagbarem

simplen wörtern wie
angst
kindergeschrei
ein poltern
düsterkeit

wörtern für meine
welt

daß ich sie hinstelle
in gedichten

daß ich sie hineinbelle
in die stille

unutterable

so full of
so filled
with things not
utterable
un-
utterable

simple words like
fear
children's cries
a din
a darkness

words for my
world

for me to confront
you with in poems

for me to bark roar grunt
into silence

das schöne bild

spar aus dem schönen bild den menschen aus
damit die tränen du, die jeder mensch verlangt
aussparen kannst; spar jede spur von menschen aus:
kein weg erinnere an festen gang, kein feld an brot
kein wald an haus und schrank, kein stein an wand
kein quell an trank, kein teich kein see kein meer
an schwimmer, boote, ruder, segel, seefahrt
kein fels an kletternde, kein wölkchen
an gegen wetter kämpfende, kein himmelsstück
an aufblick, flugzeug, raumschiff – nichts
erinnere an etwas; außer weiß an weiß
schwarz an schwarz, rot an rot, gerade an gerade
rund an rund;
so wird meine seele gesund.

the beautiful picture

withhold the human from your beautiful picture
so that you can withhold the tears for which
all human beings call; withhold the very trace:
let no path mark firm passage, no field recall bread
no forest, house or wardrobe, no stone a wall
no spring their drinking, no pond no lake no sea
a swimmer, boat, oar, sail or navigation
no rock a climber, not one little cloud
those who defy the weather, no patch of sky
an upward glance or aircraft spaceship – let
nothing recall anything, but white recall white
black, black, red, red, straight recall straight
round recall round;
so shall my soul be healed, its health be found.

glas

glas
schwester des auges
kühlerer bruder der stirn.

blume bist du in meiner hand.
als liebste kennst du meine lippen.

baum

baum
vater des tisches
ellbogenfroh.

hier, meine freunde
sind früchte
und auf gutem holz.

hand

hand
lampe des blinden
gefährtin des lieds.

du deutest den weg.
dann läßt du aufs auge dich nieder
taube der nacht.

glass

glass
sister of the eye
the forehead's cooler brother.

flower you are in my hand.
as a lover you know my lips.

tree

tree
father of the table
elbow-happy.

here, my friends
are fruits
and on good wood.

hand

hand
the blind man's lamp
the song's companion.

you point out the way.
then on the eye you settle
dove of the night.

bach

alt wie wasser
rom der libelle
bach.

wären wir fische
in deinen adern –
auch in dir
suchten wir unablässig
ein herz.

stein

jung und granit
schädel geschoren
ohne mund ohne ohr
blind

aus dem väterlichen steinbruch
mutterlos geboren
stein zu sein
bis wir staub sind.

eine mutter
gras im mund
sammelt ihr kind
unter den tischen des windes.

brook

old as water
the dragonfly's Rome
brook.

if we were fishes
within your arteries –
in you also
incessantly we should seek
a heart.

stone

young and granite
its pate shorn
without mouth without ear
blind

from the paternal quarry
born motherless
to be stone
till we are dust.

a mother
grass in her mouth
collects her child
under the wind's tables.

familie

mein vater ist kleiner als ich
meine mutter ist kleiner als mein vater
mein onkel sagte mein vater ist kleiner als meine mutter
aber mein vater ist nicht kleiner als meine mutter

mein vater ist im gegenteil größer als meine mutter gewesen
aber mein vater ist nicht tot mein onkel ist tot
mein onkel der gesagt hat mein vater ist kleiner als meine mutter
ist tot
aber mein vater ist nicht tot
aber schon lange meine mutter

nach schluß

keiner breitet ein tuch über dieses schreckliche ergebnis
aber es ist ja nicht weit und breit ein auge, vor dem es
zu verbergen gälte solchen anblick, auch sind nicht vonnöten
masken gegen die erstickenden gase; sind ja doch
lungen weit und breit, sie einzuatmen, nicht vorrätig.
und vergebens treiben die winde zu neuer schlacht, wo weit
      und breit
endlich nicht ist ein einziger feind mehr, heere des staubes.

family

my father is shorter than i am
my mother is shorter than my father
my uncle said that my father is shorter than my mother
but my father is not shorter than my mother

my father on the contrary was taller than my mother
but my mother is not dead my uncle is dead
my uncle who said my father is shorter than my mother
is dead
but my father is not dead
but my mother has been dead for a long time

after the cessation

no one throws a cloth over this terrible outcome
but there is no eye near or far from which
such a sight should be hidden. nor is there need
for masks against the suffocating gases; when lungs
near or far to inhale them are not present.
and in vain the winds incite to new battle, when near or far
at last there is not one enemy left, armies of dust.

lenin im winter

die revolution
die schneevolution
die teevolution
der schnee
der tee
die rehe

einst und jetzt

einst keiner
jetzt einer

einst und jetzt

einst einer
jetzt einer

einst und jetzt

einst einer
jetzt keiner

einst und jetzt

lenin in winter

the revolution
the snowvolution
the teavolution
the snow
the tea
the roe-deer

once and now

once none
now one

once and now

once one
now one

once and now

once one
now none

once and now

der 30. november

immer schaut man manchmal zum himmel; wieso "immer"?
jetzt ist mein vater schon sieben monate tot
und in einem monat stimmt dieser satz bereits nicht mehr;
aber in sieben jahren, falls ich lebe
war mein vater *erst* sieben monate tot,
als ich das hier schrieb.
immer schaut man manchmal zum himmel, und "immer"
ist ein zu "himmel" passendes wort, denn himmel
ist immer; daran ändern auch wolken nichts, oder :
auch die wolken sind himmel.
ich würde mich gern in gottes hand
wissen, nämlich fühlen oder denken; aber ich kenne
keinen mit dieser hand, oder kann ihn nicht erkennen.
aber die linke hand meines vaters
bewegte sich zuletzt auf der decke,
ein reiben zwischen daumen und zeigefinger,
als ob sie einander noch erkennten.
ich bewege mich schon lange nicht mehr von der stelle
und lebe ganz ohne erlebnisse.
die dinge, die ich fortließ aus meinem leben,
die ich nicht einließ,
wären jetzt meine erlebnisse.
in einem von ihnen würde ich vielleicht
meinen vater wiedererkennen, und das wäre ein erlebnis;
meines, nicht seines. für ihn
würde sich garnichts ändern. aber vorher
hätte es für ihn etwas geändert, ganz gewiß.
der punkt, an dem jede änderung
hätte *vorher* geschehen müssen, ist ein schrecklicher ort,
sobald man ihn, noch denkend und fühlend,
erreicht zu haben fürchtet. und doch
ist der himmel jetzt dunkler als zu beginn dieses schreibens
und die furcht zu gering, um jede tätigkeit zu töten.

november 30th

always one sometimes looks up to heaven; why "always"?
now my father has been dead for seven months
and in one month's time this sentence will no longer be true;
but in seven years' time, if i live
my father had been dead *only* for seven months
when i wrote these lines.
always one sometimes looks up to heaven, and "always"
is a word that fits heaven, for heaven
is always; even clouds make no difference, to that, or :
the clouds too are heaven.
i should be glad to know that i am
in god's hands, that is feel or think that; but i know
no one with such hands, or cannot recognize him.
but my father's left hand
moved at the end on the blanket,
a rubbing of thumb against forefinger
as though they still recognized each other.
for a long time i have not moved an inch
and live wholly without experiences.
the things i left out of my life,
refused to admit,
would now be experiences.
in one of these perhaps i should
recognize my father, and that would be an experience;
mine, not his. for him
nothing at all would change. but earlier
it would have changed something for him, undoubtedly.
the point where every change
ought to have occurred *earlier* is a terrible place.
as soon as, still thinking and feeling,
one fears one has reached it. and yet
heaven is darker now that it was when i started to write this
and the fear not great enough to kill off all action.

schaukelstuhl

zum siebzigsten geburtstag
vielleicht einen schaukelstuhl
nein wir werden besser tun
ihm eine geflochtene
zielscheibe zu kaufen
mit wurfpfeilen wie es die
engländer tun
in ihren pubs.
das wird ihn gesellig halten
jedenfalls nicht ruhen lassen.
das kommt ohnedies
früh genug.

wie man berge versetzt

wie man berge versetzt
weiß ich nicht
aber wie man sich verletzt
weiß ich genau.
es ist mir oft genug passiert.
einmal vielleicht sogar beim versuch
einen berg zu versetzen.
manche leute versuchen sogar
zwerge zu versetzen!
die sind meist ganz schön bissig . . .

rocking chair

for my seventieth birthday
perhaps a rocking chair
no we should do better
to buy him a plaited
target with darts like
those the english use
in their pubs.
that will keep him sociable
or at least not idle.
as for the rest in any case
this comes soon enough.

how one moves mountains

how one moves mountains
i do not know
but how one injures oneself
i know exactly.
it's happened to me often enough.
once perhaps even while trying
to move a mountain.
some people even try
to move dwarfs!
most of these can be relied on to bite . . .

wie verrückt

wie verrückt arbeiten alle an neuen romanen und
wie verrückt an neuen theaterstücken und wie
verrückt an neuen gedichten und die maler
malen wie verrückt an ihren neuen bildern und
die bildhauer hämmern wie verrückt auf ihren stein
und die komponisten tragen wie verrückt ihre häßlichen
    noten ein
und die musiker tag und nacht blasen wie verrückt
    in ihr saxophon
ihre trompete ihre posaune klarinette flöte oboe fagott

alternder dichter

nicht immer werden sie mir
alles geschriebene aus den händen reißen
um es zu drucken
sondern sie werden über mich hinwegsehen
über meinen kopf weg nach anderen spähen
und ich werde sie verstehen

ach wie klein ich geworden bin
werde ich mir sagen
keinem verstellt meine stirn mehr den blick
ich bin sehr in mich zusammengesunken
mir ist so bang

like mad

like mad everyone's working on a new novel and
like mad on new plays and like
mad on new poems and the painters
paint away like mad at their new pictures and
the sculptors hammer away like mad at their stone
and the composers like mad fill in their ugly notes
and the musicians by day by night blow like mad
into their saxophone
their trumpet their trombone clarinet flute oboe bassoon

aging poet

not for ever will they tear
everything i have written out of my hand
in order to print it
but they will overlook me
over my head will look out for others
and i shall understand

oh, how small i've become
i shall tell myself
my forehead no longer blocks anyone's gaze
so much i have collapsed into myself
it frightens me

diese gedichte

diese gedichte
sind fürchterlich
das sagt er
und das sage ich

meine er meine
meine ich seine
meine er seine
meine ich ebenfalls seine

diese gedichte
sind fürchterlich
das sagt er
und das sage ich

meine er beide
beiden zu leide
meine zu leide
ihm nur seine ich

anruf

wie schlecht es um dich steht
erwartete ich nicht zu hören

laß dich von mir nicht stören
eh es dir besser geht

verzeihe meinen anruf bitte
er wird nicht wiederholt

stehst du erst auf festen beinen
erwarte ich deinen

these poems

these poems
are execrable
that's what he says
that's what i say

if he means mine
i mean his
if he means his
i mean his all the same

these poems
are execrable
that's what he says
that's what i say

if he means both
a fair share of pain
i to his bane
mean only his again

telephone call

that you're so very ill
i didn't expect to hear

don't let me disturb you till
you give me the all-clear

meanwhile excuse my call
it will not be repeated

when you are back on your feet
ring me, and we could meet.

die beine

so, jetzt wollen wir einmal
deine beine messen.
wie alt sind diese?
zusammen 126 jahre.
und wieviel wiegen sie?
es mag an dieser axt liegen
daß ich sie noch nie
vom rumpf gebracht.
ringsum das blut
zeugt vom bemühen.

a little english

nie würde er dabei
an schuhe für die hand denken
kaum je an "loves", he loves, she loves
auch nicht an "love", my love, i love you, do you love me?
obwohl, was er tut, wenn er sie überstreift
viel mehr an lieben erinnert als die lange reihe
vom berg- bis zum lackschuh, die er füllt
mit den tieren, die er seine füße nennt.

the legs

all right, now let's
measure your legs.
how old are they?
in toto, 126 years.
and how much do they weigh?
it could be because of this axe
that i've never yet
severed them from the torso.
but the blood around them
proves that i've tried.

a little english

never they'd make him think
of shoes for the hand
rarely of loves, he loves, she loves
nor yet of love, my love, i love, do you love me?
although what he does, when he slips them on
reminds him much more of love than the long row
of shoes from patent leather to alpine which he fills
with the animals that he calls his feet.

(Translator's note: the German word for "gloves" is "Handschuhe" –
hand-shoes)

verrottetes brot

verrottetes brot
esse ich mich
etwas, das aus der erde kam
glühend wachsend
grünend rot

der bäcker bröselt die maus in den teig
und ich bin tot, ja
totes brot

die milch

die milch ist am boden
was hat die milch dort zu suchen
sie hat nichts zu suchen
aber sie zahlt es dir heim
was denn
sie rächt die kuh

rotten bread

rotten bread
i eat myself
something that came out of the earth
glowingly growing
greeningly red

the baker crumbles the mouse into the dough
and i am dead, yes
dead bread

the milk

the milk is on the floor
what business has milk to be there
it has no business
but it's paying you back
for what
it's avenging the cow

korrespondenz

so schreibe ich nur noch karten
auf denen ein ja oder ein nein
anzukreuzen ist
briefe schreibe ich nicht mehr.
wenn ich dadurch einen freund verliere
bestand diese freundschaft nur aus papier
von dem ich ohnedies genug besitze.

correspondence

so now i write only postcards
on which a yes or no
is to be marked with a cross
i no longer write letters.
if that means the loss of a friend
that friendship was made only of paper
of which anyway i have quite enough

rekorde

als ich klein war
wollte ich groß werden
wie mein vater
1 meter 64
war sein rekord

als ich erwachsen war
wie mein vater
war mein rekord
1 meter 72

1 meter 70 messe ich
laut meinem reisepaß
vom 6. februar 1991

er gilt
bis zum 6. februar 2001
meinem nächsten rekordjahr

records

when i was small
i wanted to be tall
as my father
1 metre 64
was his record

when i was grown up
like my father
my record was
1 metre 72

i metre 70 is my height
according to my passport
of february 6th 1991

it remains valid
till february 6th 2001
my next record year

peter und die kuh

jetza samma scho a bisl oet
und a scho recht koet
owa boid weamma gonz koet sein
owa goa nimma oet

(jetzt sind wir schon bißchen alt
und auch schon recht kalt
aber bald werden wir ganz kalt sein
aber gar nicht mehr alt)

amoe wird aus mir wos aussespringen
wos in mia niemoes dringwen is
und wiad auffefoan in himmö
und i wia davon nix wissn

(einmal wird aus mir etwas herausspringen
das in mir niemals dringewesen ist
und wird hinauffahren in den himmel
und ich werde davon nichts wissen)

waunsas wissn woiz   sai greiz
woraus hoez   und bei an jedn hommaschlog
hods eam grissn   und gschrian hoda
wauns es ned von söwa   gwusd haum soiz

(wenn ihr es wissen wollt   sein kreuz
war aus holz   und bei jedem hammerschlag
hat es ihn gerissen   und geschrien hat er
wenn ihr es nicht von selbst   gewußt haben sollt)

(<u>note</u>: *these poems are written in Viennese dialect; the second version
is in standard German*)

76

from peter and the cow

now we've grown a bit old
and also pretty cold
but soon we'll be cold all over
but no longer old at all

one day something will jump out of me
that was never inside me
and will rise up to heaven
and i shall know nothing about it

if you want to know   his cross
was of wood   and at each hammer blow
it tore into him   and he cried out
just in case   you didn't know that yourselves

o christenheit, du wahres

o christenheit, du wahres
überbleibsel aus einer verlorenen
einer vernichteten zeit. wie ich da saß
am waldesrand, an fichtenzapfen kauend
und neben mir, strahlend, die eingehüllte mutter
in der schale eines frühen, schamhaften bade-dresses
mit dem sie verleugnete, auf dieser
fotografie meines vaters, was über mich
den unrein geborenen sohn einst kommen
sollte. oh ich werde verrückt mit all
diesen leichen im kopf : mutter, vater
und bruder robi, angegriffen und begraben
und ich hüpfe noch, auf beinen kaum mehr gehfähig
hüpfe noch, nach dem erstinfarkt, mit meinem verquarkten
herzen.

o christendom, thou true

o christendom, thou true
relic of a lost
of an annihilated time. how i sat there
at the forest's edge, nibbling at fir-cones
and next to me, radiant, my wrapped-up mother
in the shell of an early bashful bathing-suit
with which she denied, on this
photograph of my father's, what was to befall
me the impurely born son
later, oh i am going mad with all
these corpses in my head : mother, father
and brother roby, afflicted and buried
and i still hopping about, on legs that can hardly walk,
still hopping, after the first thrombosis, with my messed-up
heart.

The Dedalus Press POETRY EUROPE series

1 : **SORGEGONDOLEN** : *The Sorrow Gondola*
Tomas Tranströmer : (Sweden) translated by *Robin Fulton*

2 : **DINGFEST** : *Thingsure*
Ernst Jandl : (Austrian) translated by *Michael Hamburger*